MEDIEVAL PARKS OF EAST YORKSHIRE

Susan Neave

Centre for Regional & Local History, University of Hull
and the Hutton Press
1991

Published by the Centre for Regional and Local History,
University of Hull
and the Hutton Press Ltd.
130 Canada Drive, Cherry Burton, Beverley
East Yorkshire HU17 7SB

Printed and bound by
Clifford Ward & Co. (Bridlington) Ltd.
55 West Street, Bridlington, East Yorkshire
YO15 3DZ

ISBN 1 872167 11 X

CONTENTS

Acknowledgements … … … … … … … … … … … … … … … … … … … 4

Introduction … … … … … … … … … … … … … … … … … … … 5

The management and economy of a park … … … … … … … … … … … … … … … … 7

Emparking and the local community … … … … … … … … … … … … … … … … 11

Parks and the landscape … … … … … … … … … … … … … … … … … … 14

Gazetteer … 17

Note on principal primary sources … … … … … … … … … … … … … … … … 58

Select bibliography … … … … … … … … … … … … … … … … … … 59

ACKNOWLEDGEMENTS

My thanks are due to the following:

The owners of records who made these available for consultation, and the staff of the archives offices and libraries where relevant material was consulted.

The many people who provided additional material or assistance, or gave permission to visit park sites, in particular Dr. and Mrs. Ashwin of Londesborough Park, Professor M. Beresford, Mr. R. A. Bethell of Rise Park, Dr. Barbara English, Dr. N. V. Jones, Jennifer Kaner, Dr. Richard Morris, Barbara and James Needham, Dr. R. Spence and John Wood.

Wendy Munday of Humberside Polytechnic, for drawing the maps which appear on pages 6 and 18.

Special thanks are due to my husband David for his advice and support.

INTRODUCTION

The word park, derived from the Old English *pearroc*, simply means a paddock or enclosed field, but in the medieval period it was more specifically used to denote a private enclosure in which deer were kept. The medieval deer park most commonly comprised an enclosed tract of wild, semi-wooded country, sometimes taken in from waste ground on the edge of a manor, and differed greatly in appearance from the landscaped parks of the 18th and 19th centuries. It is the history of the former, in both the medieval period and beyond, with which this study is primarily concerned.

It has been estimated that at least 1900 parks were established in England during the course of the Middle Ages. Although the heaviest concentration was in the midlands and south, documentary evidence relating to almost fifty medieval parks in the East Riding of Yorkshire has been found, with indications that there were probably many more. The earliest references date from the 12th century, when parks at Burstwick in Holderness, and Etton, near Beverley, are recorded. However, the major period of emparking in England occurred in the 13th and 14th centuries, and it is at this time that many East Riding parks were established. The most extensive parks in the Riding, and those for which there is most information available, were created and maintained by the great landowners. These include parks at Burstwick, which was in royal ownership; at Beverley and Bishop Burton, both owned by the Archbishop of York; at Howden, where the park was held by the Bishop of Durham; and at Catton, Leconfield, Newsholme and Wressle, all medieval estates of the Earl of Northumberland.

Deer were considered the property of the Crown, and in theory a royal licence to empark was required. The large number of well-documented parks for which no licence appears to have been granted suggests, however, that one was not necessarily sought, except where a proposed park lay close to, or within, a royal forest. Grants of licence to empark were occasionally made by the.Crown as a means of rewarding an official for services rendered, or simply as a way of indicating royal favour. During the reign of Henry II, a royal licence was granted to Thomas de Etton, under the terms of which he was allowed to 'have and hold his park, which he had made in his lands at Etton, just as he had enclosed it, well wholly and in peace'.[1] The wording suggests that the park had been enclosed at an earlier date, and that the licence was granted to offer Thomas de Etton a secure title to his land.

The distribution of parks across the Riding was far from even. A national survey suggests that the location of medieval parks closely corresponds with areas of woodland recorded in Domesday Book in 1086, and the pattern of emparking in the East Riding supports this view. Much of the woodland mentioned in Domesday Book lay on the western edge of the Riding, in the area between the Ouse and Derwent rivers. Woodland was also recorded around Beverley, on the western side of the Hull river, and in other scattered areas including parts of Holderness. There was apparently no woodland on the higher lands in the northern part of the Riding. The majority of medieval parks were established in the lower-lying areas of the Riding where the Domesday woodland was recorded, with a concentration in the area of the former royal forest of Ouse and Derwent, which was disafforested during the reign of Henry III.

The popularity of deer parks declined as the Middle Ages drew to a close. Only a handful of new parks were created in the East Riding in the 15th and 16th centuries, and many of the existing parks were abandoned around this time. In particular the changes in ownership of monastic and Church lands brought about by the Reformation marked the end of many deer parks. Economic factors and changes in fashion also played a part. On many large estates deer gave way to cattle as landowners lost interest in their parks and found it more profitable to lease out the land. Although some deer parks were recreated as part of the renewed enthusiasm for hunting in the years following the Restoration, it was not until the 18th century that a new wave of emparking spread across England. At this date the gentry began to move away from the low-lying parts of the East Riding where many of the old parks were to be found, and established new estates on the uplands. Landowners such as the Sykes of Sledmere were responsible for much planting, and for creating the landscaped parks that became such a feature of the countryside from the mid 18th century. The emphasis of parks shifted from the economic use of land to the creation of a landscape pleasing to the eye. Although these new landscaped parks often contained deer, this was no longer their prime function.

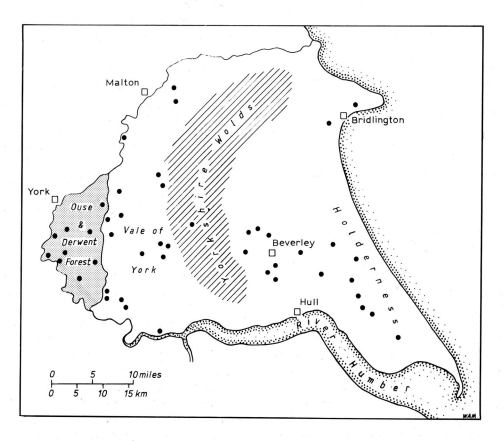

Distribution of East Riding deer parks established before 1500
(Source: see Gazetteer)

6

THE MANAGEMENT AND ECONOMY OF A PARK

Two main types of deer were kept in parks in the Middle Ages; red deer, which were native to England, and fallow deer which had almost certainly been introduced or reintroduced into the country by the Normans. Deer required a varied habitat, as this extract from *The Countrey Farm*, published in 1616, illustrates.

> Nor ought the park consist of one kind of ground only, as all of wood, all grass, or all coppice, but of divers, as part high wood, part grass or champion, and part coppice or underwood or thick spring, nor must these several grounds lie open, or as it were in common with another; but they must be separated one from the other by a strong rail through which deer or sheep (but no greater cattle) may pass, for they must have the full liberty of the place.[2]

It was the duty of a park keeper to look after the deer, ensure that the surrounding 'pale' or fence was kept in good repair, and possibly also to manage the woodland within the park. In the early medieval period these duties were sometimes performed in exchange for a landholding; at Burstwick in 1260 Simon Colin held a bovate of land for the keeping of South Park. The keepers employed on the de Roos estates at Seaton Ross and Storwood were paid by the day in the 14th century, at the rate of 2d, but more commonly a park keeper received an annual stipend. Occasionally grazing rights or other privileges were granted in addition to a sum of money. At Leconfield in 1517 the deputy keeper, John Pearson, was allowed to pasture four cows and two horses in the park, and in 1552 Robert Burton and Thomas Wakefield, keepers of Beverley Park, were allowed one 'pale walk' yielding wood

valued at 10s 6d.

A well-managed deer park provided a regular supply of meat for the table and, through the selective distribution of venison, a useful means of cultivating the more influential members of local society. Venison was a highly valued commodity, since it could be obtained by gift only. William Harrison, writing in the 1570s, described deer as 'that vain commodity which bringeth no manner of gain or profit to the owner, since they commonly give away their flesh, never taking penny for the same, because venison in England is neither bought nor sold by the right owner, but maintained only for his pleasure'.[3] In 1263 the keeper of Cottingham Park, which at that date was in the ownership of Edward, Prince of Wales (the Black Prince), was ordered to take a buck from the park and present it as a gift to Adam Pund of Hull. The registers of the Archbishops of York of the early 14th century include many references to gifts of venison from their park at Beverley.

By the latter part of the 17th century it had become traditional for the Members of Parliament for the town of Beverley to retain the support of the Corporation by presenting them with venison, usually at Christmas. It was also customary for park owners to provide venison for significant local occasions, such as the manor court feast. Several of the more prominent members of the East Riding gentry distributed venison on a regular basis to other members of the county set. Although no venison lists from the medieval period have been located, several which date from the 18th century have survived. These include lists of venison to be granted from the estate of the Constable family at Everingham, and from the park of Lord Burlington and his heir, the Duke of Devonshire, at Londesborough. The social prestige of appearing on the venison list of a landowner of the status of Lord Burlington was considerable. Recipients of venison from the park at Londesborough in the 1740s ranged from members of minor county or merchant families to more substantial landowners such as Sir Edmund Anderson and Sir William St. Quintin. In June 1743 the park keeper at Londesborough was instructed that should 'the Archbishop of York be in the country he [Lord Burlington] would have you serve him with a whole buck of this season'.[4] Park owners received numerous requests for venison. In 1717 Viscount Dunbar of Burton Constable received a letter from the mayor of Hedon asking if he could have a small piece of venison for his mayoral feast, and in August 1731 the estate steward at Everingham wrote 'I am pestered above measure with peoples importunity for venison'.[5]

As well as making gifts of venison, park owners sometimes granted the privilege of the right to hunt in their parks. Contrary to popular belief, not all parks were used for hunting. Many of the smaller manorial deer parks were too densely wooded and of insufficient size for hunting to take place, and it was only the larger parks, for example those belonging to the Archbishop of York at Beverley, and to the Earl of Northumberland at Leconfield, which were used for this purpose. At Leconfield, the 365½ acre Coursing Park was described in 1577 as 'for the most part ... plain ground without any woods except at the west end

thereof certain wood grounds plenished with oaks for the relief and succour of the deer'. Belonging to this park was 'one spring or wood ground set with oaks and underwoods' which was described as 'a place of great pleasure devised for hunting with hounds'.[6] Stag hunting became less popular in the post-medieval period as the number of deer parks declined, although the sport was still practiced at Burton Constable in the early 19th century, when a herd of between 80 and 90 red deer was kept specifically for the chase.

In addition to providing deer for the chase, and venison for the table, parks were also an important source of timber. Deer were not compatible with normal woodland management, since they would eat seedling trees and young underwood. Sometimes the whole of a park would be left open for the deer, and the trees pollarded to protect regrowth, but more commonly a park would be divided into coppices which could be protected from the deer by banks and fences, until the woodland had reached a certain age. At Leconfield Park more than 40 acres of

Medieval hunting scene.

Felling trees. Parks provided an important source of timber.

underwood, in the spring or grove known as Furwest Lees, were described in 1577 as 'greatly spoiled for lack of a good fence'.[7]

Surplus timber from parks was usually sold; wood sales from Leconfield Park in 1522, for example, realised more than £42. Sales of both timber and bark (a vital product in the tanning industry for which the East Riding was noted) are recorded in the medieval records of the royal park at Burstwick in Holderness. Much of the wood obtained from parks was, however, retained for local use. At Cottingham in 1363 the park keeper was ordered to deliver four oaks to repair bridges in the village. Parks which had been taken into Crown hands were sometimes used to supply timber for royal works. In 1537, when the Leconfield estate of the Earl of Northumberland was temporarily in the hands of the Crown, it was reported that the park there could provide sufficient timber for repairs to the quay at Bridlington, for which the Crown had assumed responsibility following the dissolution of Bridlington Priory.

A large amount of timber obtained from parks was expended on the maintenance of the surrounding pale. In the medieval period deer parks were usually enclosed by an earthen bank on the top of which was set an oak pallisade. The upkeep of the pale was one of the prime responsibilities of the park keeper. At Leconfield the emparked area was of sufficient size to merit the appointment of a 'palester' whose sole duty was to ensure that the park pale was kept in good repair. In 1577 he received an annual payment of 40 shillings, a horse to draw the sled upon which the wood used to repair the pale was carried, and the right to graze cattle in the park.

The upkeep of the park pale proved a major expense for many park owners, and in some cases may have been a contributory factor in the decision to abandon parks as deer reserves and use them solely for grazing. Damage to the pale was caused variously by bad weather, by poachers breaking into the park, or by local tenants stealing the pale boards for building-timber or firewood. Ideally trees from within a park provided the necessary timber to repair the pale, but there are many examples of parks where the management of woodland was so poor, or the quantity of timber required so great, that other sources had to be found. A Crown survey taken in 1554-5 recorded that at South Park, Burstwick, 'the pale is very good and [there is] timber enough to keep the same' but that at Newsholme Park 'the pale is clean wasted and [there is] no timber to pale it'.[8] At Wressle Park, the quantity of timber needed to repair the pale in the early 16th century was so great that it had to be imported from Carlton Wood near Snaith in the West Riding, at considerable expense.

Most parks provided grazing for stock as well as for deer, and there are numerous references to the 'agistment' (the right to graze beasts in exchange for a sum of money) of cattle, sheep and horses within parks. In 1517 the rates of agistment in the parks at Leconfield were 3s 4d for a cow, and 6s 8d for a horse. Rights of 'pannage', the feeding of swine, similarly provided income from a park. A survey of the manor of Cottingham dated 1282 refers to the 'pannage of the park and the woods'.[9] The lease of grazing rights initially provided the chief source of income from parks when deer were no longer kept, although in time large areas of previously emparked land were converted to arable.

Rights of 'pannage', the feeding of swine, were granted in many medieval parks.

EMPARKING AND THE LOCAL COMMUNITY

Although very much the preserve of the upper classes, deer parks could affect the lives of members of the local community in a variety of ways. The creation or extension of a park often encroached upon the liberties of tenants, destroying part of their common pasture or open-field land. Most devastating of all was the possibility of a whole settlement being destroyed in the course of emparking.

The evidence from the East Riding suggests that here emparking was only rarely, if ever, the cause of village depopulation in the medieval or early modern period. The hamlet of Nuthill in Holderness may have been destroyed when a park was created at Burstwick in the early Middle Ages, but no firm documentary evidence survives to confirm this. Similarly it has been suggested that the township of Raventhorpe in Cherry Burton parish may have been destroyed during the enlargement of Leconfield Park in the 16th century, but the evidence is inconclusive; part of the township's open-field land appears to have been taken into the 'New Park' of Leconfield at this time, but the site of the settlement itself clearly lies outside the boundaries of the park extension, and had probably been depopulated at an earlier date.

There is more evidence concerning the encroachment upon common pasture and open-field land at emparking. The Statute of Merton of 1236 required that compensation must be made where land over which common rights were held was involved. In 1296 an inquisition was taken concerning arable, meadow and pasture land which had been enclosed at the creation or enlargement of Totleys Park at Burstwick. An order was made that compensation should be paid in respect of these recently enclosed lands. Encroachments may have been made upon open-field land when the Archbishop of York established a park at Bishop Burton in the Middle Ages; flights of lynchets, possibly the fossilised remnants of open-field farming, can be seen within the former park. Surveys made of parks at Leconfield, Newsholme and Wressle in 1554-5 describe each of these as containing land which had formerly been arable.

The reduction in the amount of land available in England for tillage had, by the early 16th century, become a serious cause for concern. This reduction was largely attributed to the conversion of arable to pasture for sheep farming, but emparking was seen as a contributory factor. In 1517 an inquisition was taken concerning all enclosures which had been made since 1488 and in three of the surviving cases reported for the East Riding, those relating to Holme on Spalding Moor, Leconfield and Scorborough, emparking was given as the reason for enclosure.

In spite of this concern, such enclosures continued to take place throughout the 16th century. At Risby near Beverley, where the Ellerkers had established a deer park in the first half of the 16th century, several extensions were made to the park in subsequent years. In 1592 it was noted that 'the said park pale hath divers times been removed and the park enlarged' and it was reported that certain lands 'which grounds before the inclosure were parcel of Risby common corn field' had within the previous ten years been taken into the park.[10]

Discontent over the loss of land or common rights, even where compensation had been made, is often evident. At Beverley in the mid 13th century the burgesses of the town agreed to exchange certain rights of common with the Archbishop of York to enable him to create a hunting park. In spite of their agreement, many of the burgesses were afterwards dissatisfied with the exchange. The Archbishops' registers record numerous cases of trespass and poaching in the park from the 1260s onwards, most of which were clearly deliberate expressions of discontent by the burgesses rather than simply cases of common poaching. The penalty for those caught was usually excommunication. Such cases continued up to the 16th century, the most notable concerning Sir Ralph Ellerker, which was recorded in 1516. Ellerker waged a personal vendetta against the Archbishop of York, who had attempted to prevent his unlawful re-election as a governor of Beverley. In order to express his antagonism towards the Archbishop, Ellerker had trespassed in the deer park, causing considerable damage there.

Similar examples of parks trespass, often as a consequence of local feuds amongst the gentry, have been found relating to a dozen East Riding parks. The following case, recorded in the Patent Rolls for 1370, is typical.

> ... complaint by Gerard son of John Salvayn, knight, that Henry Gramary, knight, and Joan his wife, John de Barnburgh of Doncaster, Thomas Morehous, John Skelbrok, John Nanson of Skipwith, John Shepherd of North Duffield, Alan Ryffann, John Riffan and others entered his manor at North Duffield and his free warren there and at Harswell, co. York, broke his houses and the doors and windows thereof, and his park there, burned timber from the houses, hunted without licence in his warren and park, felled trees growing at North Duffield and Harswell, took away the said trees, a chest found at Harswell worth 20 shillings, with charters, writings and other muniments contained therein, a deer from the park, and hares, conies, pheasants and patridges from the warren, chasing the remaining deer from the park, have maintained themselves so far as in the manor by armed force so that his men and tenants dare not go on his land to till it ... [11]

Deer parks also offered the temptation of poaching to the lesser members of society. In 1650, for example, Christopher Smith of Hayton appeared before the Justices accused of stealing deer from Londesborough Park. Records relating to the manor of Leconfield show that here hares and rabbits were poached from the park. As well as for poaching, tenants were sometimes brought before the manor courts for breaking down the park pales.

The court rolls for Leconfield manor for 1518-19 record that four men from nearby Arram were fined 6d each for this offence. It is probable that they were simply stealing the pale wood, rather than trying to break into the park to poach. The by-laws laid down by Wressle manor court in 1569 included the clause 'none [shall] bear wood nor pale boards ... from the great park nor little park'.[12]

Animals which escaped from parks where the boundary fence was not properly maintained could cause considerable damage to surrounding farm land. The by-laws relating to Wressle manor in the mid 16th century required the park keeper and his deputy to 'make up the pales and fences about Newsham [Newsholme] park so as no cattle come forth of the same into Newsham field'.[13] A Crown survey made in 1554-5 of the vast park at Beverley, which had previously belonged to the Archbishop of York, estimated that as many as 300 deer had escaped through the broken paling into the woods outside, although it was said of those that had escaped 'they doth rest as quietly as they within the park'.[14] The problem of deer escaping from parks continued even when more sophisticated methods of enclosing parks had been devised. Early 19th century accounts for the Londesborough estate include payments to a local farmer to compensate for damage to his corn. The damage had been caused by deer which had broken through the park fence.

From the landowner's point of view, a park offered him a status symbol and an economic asset. The price he often paid for this was resentment from the local community; not merely from tenants caught poaching or aggrieved at the loss of common rights, but also from the higher ranks of society, who might use the park as a focus of attack in order to perpetuate local feuds. The deer park was not, of course, intended to be an asset to the local community, and can rarely be regarded as such. Perhaps its only benefit to the community was as a convenient poaching ground, providing, at considerable risk to the poacher, the chance of a haunch of venison for the more lowly tables of the neighbourhood.

Deer poaching

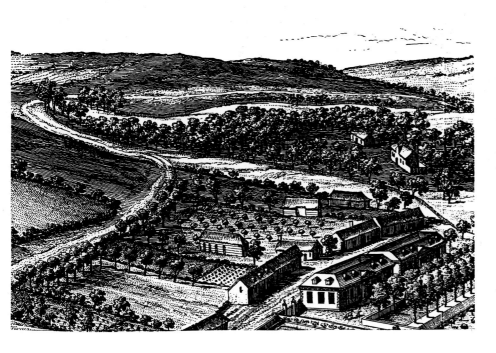

Detail from view of Londesborough by Kip and Knyff c.1700, showing park pale. The buildings within the park include the dog kennels. The 17th century stables are shown bottom right.

PARKS AND THE LANDSCAPE

Extensive records, including maps, survive relating to several of the major East Riding deer parks (for example those which belonged to the Earl of Northumberland) but many of the smaller manorial parks have left virtually no written evidence. The grant of a licence to empark, or the survival of a field or farm name incorporating the word 'park', may be the only clue that a deer park once existed. It is possible to discover the sites of many of these minor parks by examining more recent maps and aerial photographs, and undertaking fieldwork where feasible. The first edition (six inches to one mile) Ordnance Survey maps, which for the East Riding date from the mid 19th century, are especially useful. Using a combination of all the evidence available, it has been possible to determine the boundaries of approximately half the medieval parks recorded in the East Riding.

The optimum shape for a park was a circle, since this offered the maximum area of land for the minimum amount of fencing, and therefore kept the expense of maintaining the park pale as low as possible. At Beverley in the mid 16th century it was claimed that the park, which had been established in the early medieval period, could not be accurately measured in breadth at either end 'for that it is so round'.[15] The boundary of a former park sometimes survives in the form of a curvilinear hedgerow marking a block of early enclosure, surrounded by fields of a more regular shape which had been laid out at parliamentary enclosure in the 18th or early 19th century. Occasionally the boundary of a park followed that of a parish, for example, at Etton where the northern boundary of the park coincided with the boundary between the parishes of Etton and Lockington. Natural boundaries, in particular streams, were also adopted.

Where a park had a distinctive boundary, there may be a particular reason, as at Catton where the very irregular western boundary of the former park can still be traced. The pale was apparently designed to follow such a twisting course as part of a bargain made by Richard de Percy with the villagers of neighbouring Wilberfoss in the 13th century, whereby they gave up rights of common in his wood, in return for which he ensured that the boundary of his new park did not encroach upon their reclaimed arable lands. A Crown survey made in 1554-5 noted of the boundary of Catton Park that 'it cannot be well measured in length nor in breadth but yet were all measured by perch for that it goith out with so many corners'.[16]

Occasionally the boundary of a medieval park is still marked by an earthen bank, on which the oak pallisade would have been set, and by an inner ditch following the line of the bank. The best example of this type of earthwork to be found in the East Riding is at Bishop Burton where large stretches of a bank and ditch marking the boundary of the former park of the Archbishop of York survive. The bank at Bishop Burton, known as the Reins, is lined with oaks and other deciduous trees, and in Spring is carpeted with bluebells, a sign of ancient woodland. Remains of banks and ditches have been located at several other places known to have had medieval parks, notably at Howden, where a substantial stretch of bank can be traced, and less prominently at Beverley, Etton, Newsholme, Rise and Wressle. Surviving banks vary considerably in height and width; the bank at Bishop Burton is up to 25 feet in width, and five feet in height.

Other earthworks associated with deer parks include small mottes or mounds which served as look-outs. Sometimes ridge and furrow (indicating the conversion of land from arable to pasture) is found within a park boundary or, more rarely, the earthworks of an abandoned settlement. The village may, of course, have been depopulated long before emparking took place.

Many deer parks contained a grassy clearing known as a 'laund' or 'lawn' and the survival of this name can provide

The twisting boundary of Catton Park.

a clue to the former existence of a park. At Beverley in the mid 16th century it was reported that 'the laund within the same park containeth round about two miles as it was measured by the commandment of Sir Michael Stanhope when it was new paled'.[17] Former East Riding deer parks where the name 'lawn' survives to mark the site include those at Cottingham, North Duffield and Wheldrake. Another feature found within parks which has left no visible trace, but which has sometimes given its name to a close or wood, is a cockshot or cockglade. A cockshot was a net suspended across poles for the purpose of catching woodcocks. At Beverley a survey of 1552 records that 'John Francis hath made certain waste in Beverley Park in making a cockglade'.[18] There are references to cockshots in the parks of North Duffield and Leconfield; cockshot appears as a field name on an 18th century map of the area formerly covered by Leconfield Park.

In contrast to the 18th century landscaped park, the medieval park was not designed as a setting for a country house, and was often sited some distance away from a castle or manor house. This was the case at Wressle, where both the Great Park and Newsholme Park lay some distance to the north and east respectively of Wressle Castle. At Leconfield, however, the fortified manor house, the site of which is still marked by an impressive moat, lay within the park pale. Most of the larger parks contained a lodge, which commonly provided a permanent residence for the park keeper but which might also be used to accommodate hunting parties. The lodge which lay within the North Park at Burstwick in the 14th century had a hall (thatched and with a chamber at either end), a chapel, a kitchen and a stable. At Leconfield, the topographer John Leland, writing in the first half of the 16th century, noted that there was a 'fair tower of brick for a lodge in the park'.[19] When the park at Leconfield was extended and subdivided, additional lodges were built. In 1571 the lodge in the Coursing Park was described as built of timber with a tiled roof. Lodge buildings were commonly converted to farmhouses after disparking. Although no lodges have survived in the East Riding, farms continue to mark some

of their sites; at Catton, for example, the farm known as Catton Park stands on the site of a deer park lodge. At Leconfield a small moat marks the site of the lodge which stood in the New Park.

Other buildings found within parks provided shelter for animals. At Wressle repairs to the deerhouse are referred to accounts of 1542-5. A series of arches below the terrace at the site of Londesborough Hall provided shelter for the deer in the park which had been created there earlier in the 17th century; these arches are still known locally as the deer shelters.

On first appearance, medieval parks have left little imprint on the East Riding countryside. A handful survived into the 18th century, and were transformed into more fashionable landscaped parks, but the majority had been returned to agricultural land well before the close of the 17th century. With the aid of maps and aerial photographs a closer inspection does, however, reveal that many parks have left some visible clue to their former existence — an area of ancient woodland, the trace of a bank or an unusual shape to a field boundary. Many of the smaller parks were relatively short-lived, and have left virtually no documentary evidence to record their existence, but few can have left no trace at all on the landscape, however obscure.

References

(1) Hall, T. W. *Etton, an East Yorkshire Estate Village 1170-1482* (Sheffield, 1932) p.7

(2) Shirley, E. *English Deer Parks* (London, 1867) p.234

(3) Ibid p.27

(4) Chatsworth House Archives — Bolton Abbey MSS: letter book of Henry Simpson, 25 June 1743

(5) Roebuck, P. *Constable of Everingham Estate Correspondence 1726-43* Yorkshire Archaeological Society Record Series vol 136 (1976) p.45

(6) Fisher, E. J. 'Some Yorkshire Estates of the Percies' (unpublished PhD thesis, Leeds, 1953) vol 1 p.46

(7) Ibid

(8) Public Record Office [PRO] SC12 19/41

(9) Brown, W. (ed) *Yorkshire Inquisitions vol 1* Yorkshire Archaeological Society Record Series vol 12 (1892) p.240

(10) Borthwick Institute of Historical Research CP G 2654

(11) *Calendar of Patent Rolls* 1367-70 p.427

(12) West Sussex Record Office — Petworth House Archives 7191

(13) Ibid 7190

(14) PRO SC12 19/41

(15) Ibid

(16) Ibid

(17) Ibid

(18) Leeds City Archives GC FO2 f.85

(19) Woodward, D (ed) *Descriptions of East Yorkshire: Leland to Defoe* (East Yorkshire Local History Society, pamphlet no.39 1985) p.8

GAZETTEER

Although the present study is concerned primarily with parks established in the medieval period, the gazetteer has been expanded to include parks known to have been created before 1700. All are thought to have been used for keeping deer. A further list is given of places where deer parks may have existed, but where the evidence is insufficient to merit inclusion in the main gazetteer.

Landscaped parks created in the 18th and 19th centuries on estates where there is no previous history of a deer park, for example Sledmere, have not been included.

A National Grid Reference is given for each entry in the gazetteer. Where the precise location of the park is known, the reference relates to the approximate centre of the park; otherwise it refers to the general vicinity in which it is believed the park lay.

Maps showing sites of parks accompany several of the gazetteer entries. These are based on the Ordnance Survey (six inches to one mile) 1850s edition. The suggested park boundary is indicated by a black dotted line.

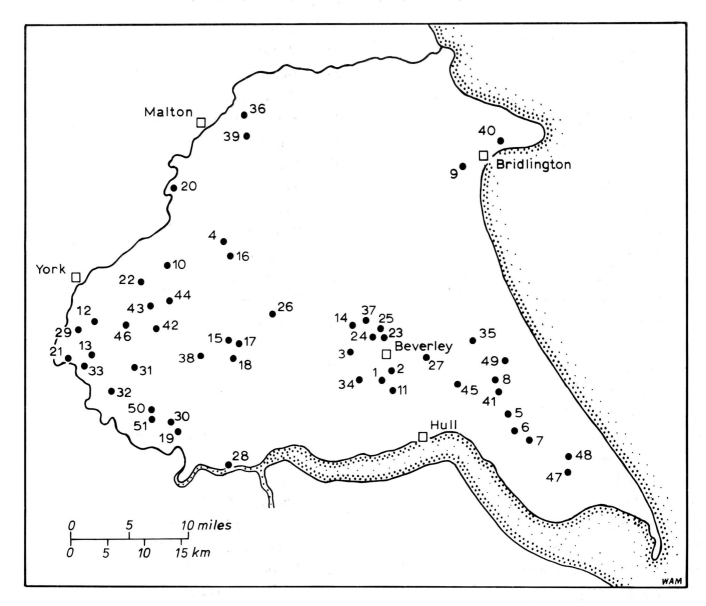

Location of parks (see accompanying key)

Key to map showing location of East Riding parks established before 1700

1	Bentley		27	Meaux
2	Beverley		28	Metham
3	Bishop Burton		29	Moreby
4	Bishop Wilton		30	Newsholme
5	Burstwick: North Park		31	North Duffield
6	: South Park		32	Osgodby
7	: Totleys Park		33	Riccall
8	Burton Constable		34	Risby
9	Carnaby		35	Rise
10	Catton		36	Scagglethorpe
11	Cottingham		37	Scorborough
12	Deighton		38	Seaton Ross
13	Escrick (Riccall Park)		39	Settrington
14	Etton		40	Sewerby
15	Everingham		41	Sproatley
16	Grimthorpe		42	Storwood
17	Harswell		43	Sutton upon Derwent
18	Holme on Spalding Moor		44	Sutton upon Derwent
19	Howden			(Woodhouse Park)
20	Howsham		45	Swine
21	Kelfield		46	Wheldrake
22	Kexby		47	Winestead: Old Park
23	Leconfield: Old Park		48	: New Park
24	: New Park		49	Withernwick (Lambwath Park)
25	: Coursing Park		50	Wressle : Great Park
26	Londesborough		51	: Little Park

BENTLEY (Rowley Parish)   TA 030 360

A small manorial deer park may have been established at Bentley c.1280 when Richard de Bentley claimed the right to keep his wood enclosed. In the 16th century Bentley Park or Wood was said to contain 44 acres. Reference to agistment of the park was made. In the 17th century Bentley Park, then described as covering almost 87 acres, was taken into an adjacent deer park at Beverley.

BEVERLEY   TA 040 370

There was a deer park at Beverley in the medieval period belonging to the Archbishop of York. In or around the year 1258 Archbishop Sewall de Bovill persuaded the burgesses of the town to exchange rights of common in the park in return for rights to land in Westwood as well as Figham, so that emparking for hunting purposes could take place. From the 1260s onwards there are frequent accounts of trespassing and poaching in the park, probably a sign of discontent among the burgesses at their loss of common rights there. In 1279-80 the Archbishop of York was required to report to the Quo Warranto commissioners by what right he held the park at Beverley. A survey dated 1388 stated that '400 beasts, counting by the short hundred, can be fed in the park over and above the sustenance of game'.

The archiepiscopal manor passed to the Crown in 1542 when Archbishop Lee exchanged it, together with the manors of Skidby and Bishop Burton, for cash and various lands and advowsons. Sir Michael Stanhope was appointed as royal keeper of the park, and in 1548 he built a lodge there, using stone from Hall Garth, the former manor house of the Archbishop of York which lay to the south of Beverley Minster. A survey taken in 1554-5 suggests that by this date the park extended right from the southern edge of the town to the southern parish boundary, covering an area of almost 2,300 acres. The park was described as six miles in circumference, two miles in length and a mile and three-quarters in breadth from 'the postern gate near Beverley unto Brodewell

corner'. The precise location of these places is unknown, although the making of a timber bar at the end of Bradwell Lane in Beverley was recorded in 1445, and in the 17th century 'Brodewell' was described as in the vicinity of Queensgate and Butt Lane, to the west of the town. The 1554-5 survey also noted that the park incorporated 800 acres of pasture which had previously been arable, accounting for the presence of ridge and furrow in the area today. The park contained 650 fallow deer, and a further 300 were estimated to have escaped through the broken paling into the woods outside. In 1574 the area was described as lately disparked.

In 1628 Beverley Parks came into the possession of the Warton family. By 1667 the Wartons had re-emparked part of the area and were keeping deer there. Their park extended into Bentley township, enclosing within its pale an area known as Bentley Park together with two closes. In 1674 six additional closes were taken into the park. The Wartons' park would appear to have been considerably smaller than that of the Archbishop of York, covering perhaps about 250 acres, of which 117 acres lay within Bentley township.

An inventory taken on the death of Michael Warton in 1688 lists 1000 pales stored at the Lodge at Beverley Parks, together with hay for the deer. In an account book of the same date a park keeper's salary is recorded. Between 1686 and 1694 Michael Warton and his son presented the Corporation of Beverley with annual gifts of venison.

It is not known when the Wartons last kept deer at Beverley Parks, but the family died out in the male line in 1725 and the estate was finally split up in 1775. Lands purchased in Beverley Parks by Joseph Dickinson in 1803-05 included nine closes collectively called Park totalling 118 acres.

The area covered by the medieval park has retained the name Beverley Parks, and traces of a bank and ditch on the western boundary have been found.

Suggested boundary of medieval park at Beverley, superimposed on Ordnance Survey map of 1855.

(A) Park Lodge.
(B) Probable position of Bentley Park.
(C) Cottingham Park.

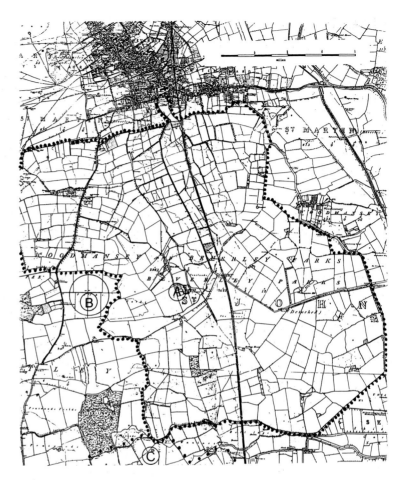

Beverley Park from plan of Yorkshire, 1720, by John Warburton.

BISHOP BURTON   SE 985 404

Like that at Beverley, the medieval park at Bishop Burton belonged to the Archbishop of York. The earliest reference to the park dates from 1323 when it was said to have been broken into and deer taken. A survey of the manor of 'Southburton' (Bishop Burton) dated 1388 refers to the felling of oaks within the park. At this date agistment of the park was said to be worth '46s 8d yearly clear besides the sustenance of the game'. A pasture called New Park was mentioned. Reference was also made to the park ditch, which, together with a substantial bank known as the Reins, still surrounds a greater part of the park site. This was referred to as the keeper's walk in the mid 16th century.

The manor passed into the hands of the Crown in 1542, and in 1563, when reversion of a lease was granted to Christopher Estofte, 'herbage and pannage' of the park was mentioned. It is not known if deer were still kept in the park by this date. The former park now surrounds an agricultural college. The surviving boundary bank is by far the most impressive earthwork of its type in the East Riding.

BISHOP WILTON   SE 802 552

The manor of Bishop Wilton also belonged to the Archbishop of York. Although no documentary evidence for a park has been found, the field names Low Parks, High Parks and Park Head on a plan of 1765 suggest that this manor also supported a deer park, which must have been situated to the south of Hall Garth, site of the archiepiscopal manor house.

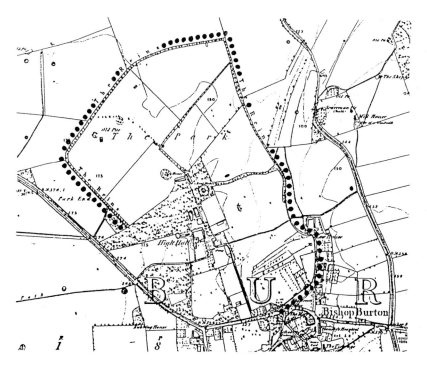

Boundary of medieval park at Bishop Burton, superimposed on Ordnance Survey map of 1855.

BURSTWICK

North Park	TA 212 315
South Park	TA 218 285
Totleys Park	TA 239 274

A park existed at Burstwick during the time of the holding of the estate by William le Gros, count of Aumale (c.1130-1179). By 1260 there were two parks, North Park and South Park. Two-thirds of the Burstwick estate passed into Crown hands in 1274, and the Crown took full possession in 1293. Robes for the keeper of the Great or North park at Burstwick are mentioned in the accounts of the Sheriffs of Holderness in the mid-late 13th century, and there are references to venison being sent to London for consumption by the royal household. In addition to keeping deer, the Crown maintained a stud at Burstwick.

In 1296 an inquisition was made concerning the taking of around 90 acres of open field land for the creation or enlargement of a third park, Totleys Park, 'which the king commanded to be made'. In the mid 14th century this park was said to cover 110 acres, and to comprise two woods and an 80 acre 'lawn'. At this date North Park covered approximately 500 acres and South Park 210 acres. There is no mention of Totleys Park after the 14th century.

In the early 14th century North Park contained a lodge. The lodge was apparently rebuilt in 1334-5 when a new lodge in South Park was also mentioned.

In 1521-2 North Park was said to contain 400 fallow deer, but South Park only 60, 'by occasion that of late it hath been destroyed wherefore time there have been and may yet be cc [200] deer'. A figure of 160 deer is recorded in 1538-9 but it is not clear if this refers to one or both of the remaining parks. The condition of South Park had improved by 1554-5 when it contained 100 fallow deer, and its pale was described as in good repair. At this date it was said to measure a quarter of a mile in length and over a quarter of a mile in breadth. In the same survey North Park was said to extend for a mile in length from north to south, and to vary in breadth from half to less than a quarter of a mile. This park contained 160 deer, but the condition of its pale was described as 'variable'.

In 1558 the Crown granted the Burstwick estate to Henry Neville, Earl of Westmorland, and in 1560 he sold it to his son-in-law, John Constable. Both North and South Parks are depicted on Lord Burghleigh's chart of the Humber dated c.1560, with deer clearly visible within the pale of the larger North Park. A survey of the Holderness estates of the Constables made in 1578 shows that at this date North Park was let to Ralph Ellerker and his wife and South Park, together with a parcel of ground known as parks underwood, was let to Christopher Metcalf. It is not known whether deer were still kept in North Park after the 16th century, but when the Constable lands were sequestrated during the Civil War it was specified that the new occupant of South Park should preserve the deer there. The will of the keeper of South Park was proved in 1661.

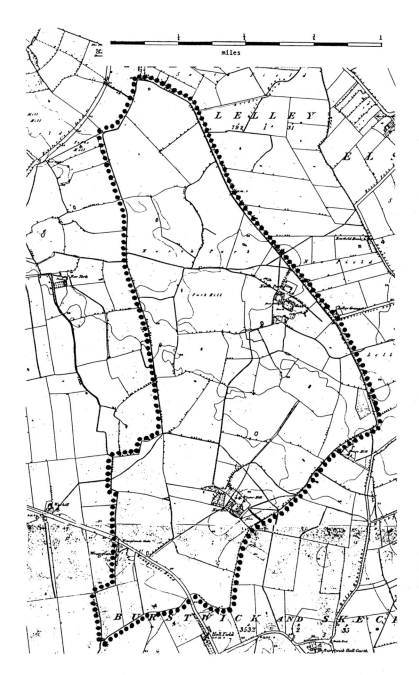

North Park, Burstwick – boundary based on a plan of 1774, superimposed on Ordnance Survey map of 1855.

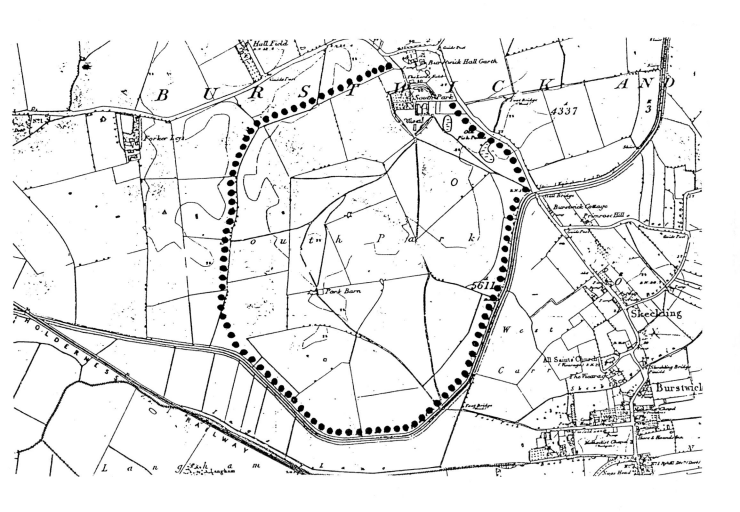

South Park, Burstwick – boundary based on a plan of 1774, superimposed on Ordnance Survey map of 1855.

BURTON CONSTABLE (Aldbrough parish) TA 190 366

The earliest park at Burton Constable may have covered only the 35 acres described as 'Old Park' in a survey of 1578. By this date a very much larger deer park had been established, which was said to contain 'plenty of fallow deer and red to the quantity of the ground which contains ccclxxxiiii [384] acres and ii [2] roods'. This park, which lay to the west of the Constable family's manor house, probably comprised the areas named on a plan of 1621 as Old Park, the Frith, the Leas, Broom and Backhouse Field, which together totalled 380 acres. A painting of the late 17th century shows deer in these areas to the west of the house. The presence of ridge and furrow suggests that some of the land taken into the park was formerly arable.

Deer were still kept at Burton Constable in the early 18th century. The park was altered later in the 18th century as part of the landscaping of the grounds of Burton Constable Hall, but a herd of deer was retained. The stock of deer was given as 240 in 1766. Venison accounts from 1766 to 1865 survive. Paintings of the late 18th century continue to show deer in the area to the west of the house. By 1840 the number of deer had increased to an estimated 500 fallow deer within the park, together with 80 or 90 red deer kept in paddocks and reserved for the chase. In 1867 Burton Constable park was said to cover 290 acres, and to house approximately 160 red deer together with 350 fallow deer 'of all colours'. The herd may have been dispersed around 1880; in February of that year Sir William Quintin of Scampston was advised that 'There is a young red stag deer, also a hind about three or four years old still for sale at Burton Constable price £20 ... you could also have two dark fallow bucks at £4 each on the same terms'. No later references to deer at Burton Constable have been found.

Burton Constable Park from a plan of Yorkshire, 1720, by John Warburton.

Burton Constable Park from a plan of Yorkshire, 1775, by Thomas Jefferys.

CARNABY
TA 150 650

A survey of the manor of Walter de Heslerton at Carnaby made in 1368 includes a reference to a park. An area to the south of the village is still known as the Parks.

CATTON
SE 730 520

A park was established at Catton by Richard de Percy in the 13th century and a reference of 1352 shows that deer were kept there. Little more is known of the history of the park during the medieval period. In 1512 it was said to contain 79 deer. A Star Chamber case of the late 1520s concerned the keeper of Catton Park who had been dismissed by Henry Percy, Earl of Northumberland, following accusations that he had felled wood and destroyed deer in the park.

In 1538, when the park was described as two miles in circumference, and well paled, it contained only 30 deer. Repairs to a park lodge are recorded at various times between 1538 and 1545. When the park was surveyed in 1554-5, the stock of deer had increased to 100. The dimensions of the park were given as half a mile in length and a quarter of a mile in breadth, but it was noted that it could not be easily measured because the pale followed such a sinuous route. This was a result of an agreement made at emparking that the boundary of the park would not encroach upon arable land which had been reclaimed from the woodland.

By 1577 the park pale was described as 'in very great decay and is of necessity to be repaired if any deer shall be kept therein'. Only 24 deer remained within the park. A keeper's lodge, described as covered with tile and slate, and with stables and outhouses adjoining, was mentioned, and within the park were seven springs or groves of wood. Between 1577 and 1601 more than a thousand oak trees were felled within the park. The timber was used to carry out work at the court house in Catton, mills at Stamford Bridge and for repairs to the park lodge and pale. By 1602 one of the springs or groves had been converted to an arable close and let to a tenant. Disparking had taken

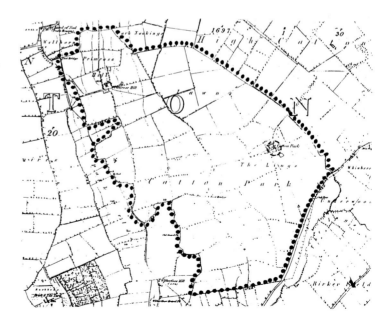

Catton Park – boundary based on a plan of 1616, superimposed on Ordnance Survey map of 1854.

(Continued on page 30)

The medieval bank, known as the Reins, which marks the boundary of the deer park of the Archbishop of York at Bishop Burton.

Series of 17th century brick arches below the terrace at the site of Londesborough Hall. The arches were used as deer shelters.

The medieval manor house of the Bishop of Durham at Howden. The episcopal deer park lay north-west of the town.

place by 1616; a map of this date shows the former park divided into closes.

The twisting course which the pale followed on the western edge of the park has been preserved in field boundaries, and remnants of the bank which surrounded the park are discernible. The farm known as Catton Park stands of the site of the park lodge.

COTTINGHAM   TA 040 343

A park at Cottingham is first mentioned in 1241. In a survey of the manor made in 1282, following the death of Baldwin Wake, the park is described as well enclosed, four leagues in circuit and containing sufficient pasture to support 500 deer. Underwood and pannage of the park are mentioned. In 1361 the park passed by marriage into the hands of Edward, Prince of Wales (the Black Prince). In 1364 he appointed his clerk to hunt there, and to have the venison salted and sent to Aquitaine. In the same year he ordered that the park was to be enclosed with pales towards the Northwood, and 'deer leaps' made. This suggests that the park pale had fallen into disrepair at this point, the purpose of the deer leaps being to encourage escaped deer to re-enter the park. A deer leap enabled an animal to enter a park but once inside there was no means of getting out again.

By the 15th century the manor of Cottingham had been subdivided into four separate manors, known as Powis, Richmond, Sarum and Westmorland. All the manors except Powis held shares in the park; in lieu of a share in the park Powis held the adjoining 100 acre 'laund'. Disparking may have taken place in or before the 16th century. Richmond Park was described as decayed by 1610, and the other parks appear to have been divided into closes by the 17th century.

The emparked area stretched almost from the centre of Cottingham village to the northern boundary of the parish, and occupied about 500 acres. The area still retains the name Cottingham Parks.

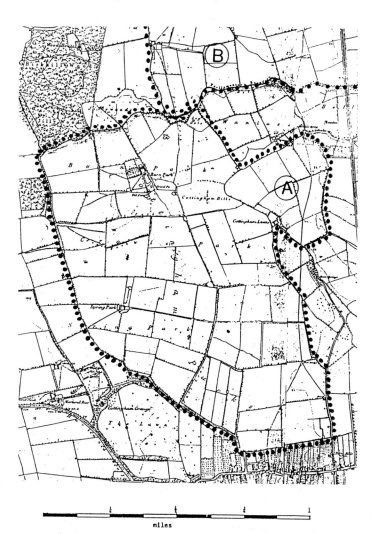

Cottingham Park – boundary based on a plan of c.1600, superimposed on Ordnance Survey map of 1855. (A) The Laund   (B) Beverley Park.

DEIGHTON (Escrick parish)

SE 618 437

The enclosing of a park at Deighton by the abbot of St. Mary's Abbey, York is recorded in the Hundred Rolls of 1276. In 1517 reference was made to a surrounding ditch, and substantial ditches are still to be found on the northern and eastern boundaries of the former park. The possessions of St. Mary's Abbey passed to the Crown at the Reformation. A wood called Deighton Park was included in a survey of royal woodland made in 1543. Timber from the wood was used for repairs to the pale of Leconfield Park. At this date the wood, presumably the former park, contained about 100 acres.

The boundaries of the emparked area are shown on a map of Deighton dated 1619. The modern Parks Farm lies at the eastern edge of the former deer park.

ESCRICK (RICCALL PARK)

SE 623 395

In addition to the enclosure of a park at Deighton in Escrick parish, the Hundred Rolls of 1276 record the enclosure of a park by the abbot of St. Mary's Abbey within the township of Escrick. In 1343 damage by flooding, caused by neglect to the banks of a sewer, was said to have affected 50 acres of land there, and in 1362 the repair of a track running alongside the park was the subject of a law suit. Common rights in the park were mentioned in the mid 15th century. Following the dissolution of St. Mary's Abbey in 1539 the park, like that at Deighton, was taken into Crown hands. It was apparently known as Riccall Park by that date. There is no connection with the park of the Bishop of Durham in the parish of Riccall. A survey of the king's woodland indicates that timber from Riccall Park was used both for repairs to the pale of Leconfield Park and for work on the King's Manor at York. The park, described by this date as a wood, was estimated to be three miles or more in circumference. In 1552 it was said that the fences of the wood called Riccall Park had been open for two years to the 'great loss of the kings woods' but that they had since been repaired.

A map of c.1600 enables the boundaries of the former park to be determined. This map shows that the park lay in the south-west corner of Escrick parish, ajoining Riccall parish, which may be why it became known as Riccall Park. Most of the western edge of the former park is bounded by a stream, lined with oak trees, and on the northern boundary a ditch, also lined with mature oaks, can be traced.

A landscaped park, which was created by the Thompson family (later Lords Wenlock) at Escrick following enclosure in 1781, lay in a different part of the parish, and there is no connection between that park and the medieval park described above.

ETTON

SE 992 445

The earliest reference to a park at Etton occurs during the reign of Henry II (1154-89) when Thomas de Etton was licensed to hold the deer park he had enclosed there. In 1316 the boundaries of the park were described as 'the field of Etton next Lockyngton as it lay in length and breadth by the moor of Etton on the west, towards the meadow of John Danyel and the field of Belagh on the east and by the land and wood, which formerly were of the Templars on the south, as far as the field of Lockyngton on the north, with the dikes which enclosed it'. There were arable enclosures within the park at this date. Later in the 14th century the park became known as Lawrence Park, after its then owner Lawrence de Etton. It is uncertain how long it continued as a deer park, but composition for the tithes of Etton Park was paid in 1685 and disparking had almost certainly taken place by this date.

The probable boundaries of the former park, which lay in the north-east corner of Etton parish, can be determined using the 14th century description. Traces of a bank and ditch are still visible on the western boundary.

A further 'park' at Etton was mentioned in 1227 when a wood called 'le Parc' belonged to the Knights Templars. It is unlikely, however, that this was used for keeping deer. The Templars were suppressed in 1312. Temple Wood and Temple Park are mentioned in the 14th century.

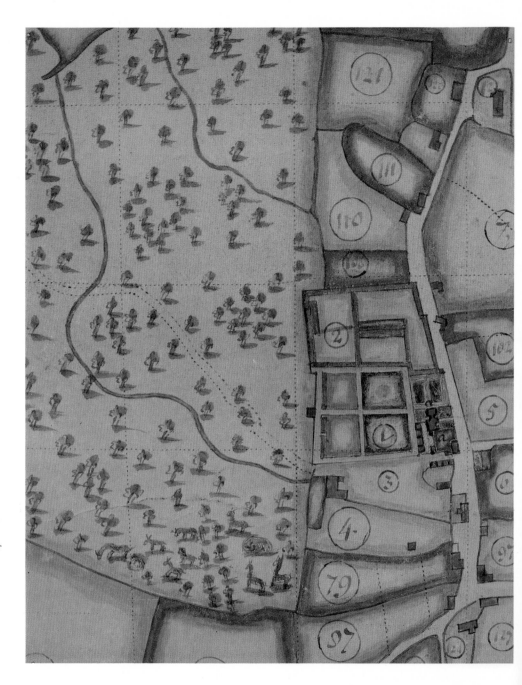

Detail from plan of Rise, 1716, showing deer in the park. (By kind permission of R.A. Bethell. Photograph by University of Hull Photographic Service).

Wressle from the air, showing the remains of the 14th century castle of the Earl of Northumberland. The deer park known as the North or Great Park occupied the top third of the photograph. A smaller park adjoined the castle.
(Photograph by Richard Morris).

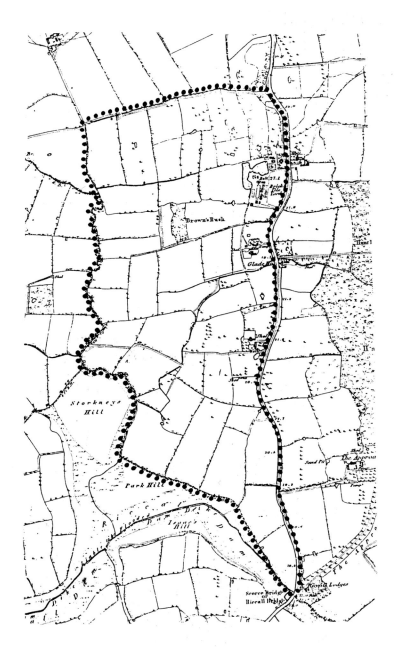

Escrick – boundary of Riccall Park, based on a plan of c.1600, superimposed on Ordnance Survey map of 1851.

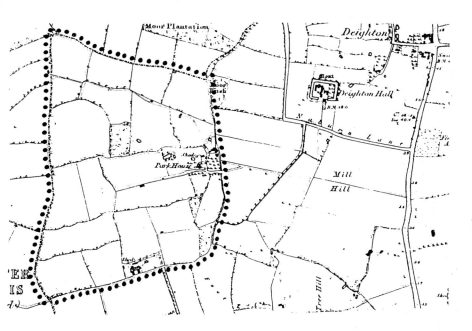

Deighton Park – boundary based on a plan of 1619, superimposed on Ordnance Survey map of 1851.

Suggested boundary of Etton Park, superimposed on Ordnance Survey map of 1855.

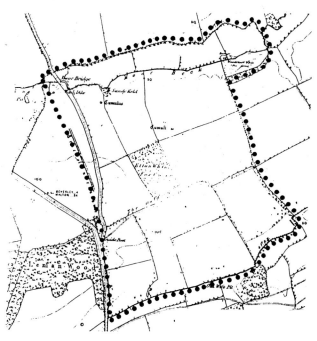

EVERINGHAM
SE 810 420

References to a park at Everingham occur in inquisitions taken in 1268 and 1287. Nothing more is known of the park during the medieval period but it was still in existence or had been re-emparked by 1577 when it is shown on Saxton's map of the East Riding. In 1635 a survey of the manor of Everingham described the demesne lands as including a park adjoining the house 'which hath sometimes been in many divisions but now lieth all together and containeth 378 acres 2 roods 20 perches'. In 1687 Sir Philip Constable applied for a licence to enable himself and his heirs to 'keep up the said park and store it with deer'. The park was described as having existed 'time out of mind'.

In 1702 Sir Philip Constable leased the park to Francis Stanfield of York, but reserved the right to pasture and agistment for 50 deer and five horses. A condition of the lease was that Stanfield should provide hay in the winter for the deer. At that date the number of deer exceeded 50, and Constable agreed to pay ten shillings a year in respect of each of the additional deer until he was able to reduce the herd to the agreed number.

Estate correspondence of the early and mid 18th centuries provides a useful insight into the management of the park which in 1734 was said to contain around 400 deer. It was still well stocked in 1892 when the herd was numbered at 200. Everingham Hall was taken into military occupation during the Second World War and the remaining deer are said to have escaped from the park at this time.

GRIMTHORPE (Great Givendale parish)
SE 813 529

The manor of Grimthorpe was held by the Fitzwilliam family in the 14th century, and on the death of Ralph Fitzwilliam in 1323 his widow Alice was assigned it as part of her dower. She afterwards married Ralph Lord Neville of Raby. An inquisition taken following her death in 1375 includes a survey of Grimthorpe Manor, in which

reference to 'a park with deer' is made. No subsequent references to this park have been found.

HARSWELL
SE 823 408

In 1370 Thomas de Roos complained that his park at Harswell had been broken into, hunted in without licence, trees felled and deer taken. A plan of Harswell dated 1605 shows areas named 'deer lawnd', 'deare lawnd wood' and 'park'. The latter was described as arable indicating that disparking had taken place by this date. A farm in the area is known as Park Farm, and faint traces of bank at the eastern edge of the former 'deare lawnd wood' may represent part of the park boundary.

HOLME ON SPALDING MOOR
SE 815 394

A park keeper at Holme on Spalding Moor is referred to in a document dated between 1223 and 1245. A reference to William Constable's 'park of Nord Schot in Holm' occurs c.1260. In 1365 Marmaduke Constable accused certain local people of taking deer and driving away cattle from his park. Ten acres of land were enclosed to enlarge the park at Holme on Spalding Moor sometime between 1488 and 1517. This extension to the original park may have been the 'New Park' referred to a survey of woodlands made in 1552, and again in a deed of 1566.

An area of old enclosure (in the northern part of Holme parish), called Park Closes on the enclosure plan of 1774, marks the site of the former park. A moated site (now destroyed) which lay within this area may have been that of a hall or park lodge.

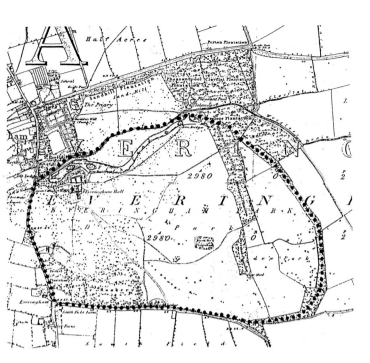

*Boundary of Everingham Park,
superimposed on Ordnance Survey map
of 1855.*

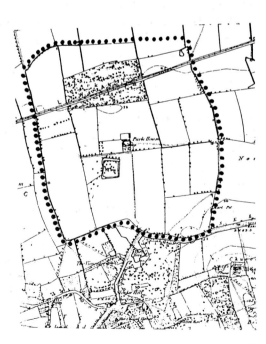

*Suggested boundary of Holme on Spalding Moor Park, based
on enclosure plan of 1774, superimposed on Ordnance Survey
map of 1854.*

HOWDEN
SE 743 295

Reference to the enclosing of a park at Howden by the Bishop of Durham is made in 1241. Little is known of its early history, but the accounts of the receiver and stock keeper of the Bishop of Durham in the 15th and 16th centuries include references to income from the lease of the herbage of the park and Lawns, and from the sale of firewood. Annual payments to a park keeper are recorded. In 1518-19 £6 11s 8d was spent on repairs to the park pale and in the 1530s and 1540s regular payments were made for dressing the park ditches. A Star Chamber case of the early 1530s shows that Howden Park still contained deer at this date, but when the Yorkshire residences of the Bishop of Durham were surveyed in 1561 the surveyors recorded that at Howden 'There is a park, wherein no deer'. The park, estimated to be 'a mile and a half about' was leased out at this date. Annual payments to a park keeper continued to be made until the 1630s but the post was probably only a sinecure. A parliamentary survey of the Bishop of Durham's estate at Howden was made in 1648 when it was noted by the surveyors 'We know of no free warren the Lord hath in his manor except that part of the demesnes now called the park and which anciently was a park well stored with deer and very full of wood and timber now utterly destroyed'.

Leases relating to the episcopal manor house and associated lands from 1676 to 1833 refer to an area known as the Parks, almost certainly the area which had formerly been the deer park. From 1737 this area is described as being divided into 14 closes (including Old Lawn Close) which together totalled 273 acres. The boundaries of the parks are given as Barnehill Lane on the west, Howden Common on the north, Knedlington Lane to the south, with closes lying in the east. Parts of the boundary bank of the former deer park can still be traced, in particular on the northern and western boundaries where a tree-covered bank of approximately 25 feet in width, with a shallow ditch on either side, survives. There is no trace of the lodge which once stood by the park gate, and which in 1577 was said to be in a very ruinous state, but in Howden itself, half a mile from the former park, the medieval manor house of the Bishop of Durham has recently been restored.

HOWSHAM (Scrayingham parish)
SE 735 630

The manor of Howsham was held by the de Roos family in the 13th century. The earliest reference to a park is in 1285 when the pasture of the park was said to be worth 40 shillings. A manorial survey dated 1352 refers to deer in the park. In 1363 Thomas de Roos complained that his park at Howsham had been broken into and deer taken. No further references to the medieval park have been found.

Considerable changes took place at Howsham in the second half of the 18th century when extensive work was carried out to the surroundings of Howsham Hall, then home of Nathaniel Cholmley. The changes included the removal of much of the village and the creation of a new parkland landscape, but no record of deer being kept at Howsham in the post-medieval period has been found.

KELFIELD (Stillingfleet parish)
SE 595 385

In 1311 Henry son of Conan was granted a licence to hold his woods at Kelfield enclosed and emparked as his ancestors had done. No further references to the park have been found.

KEXBY (Catton parish)
SE 703 494

In 1334 Thomas Ughtred was granted a licence to empark his woodland at Kexby. The park had probably been disparked by the 17th century when documents refer to closes around the Old Hall called 'Plane of the Parke' and 'Lady Parkes'.

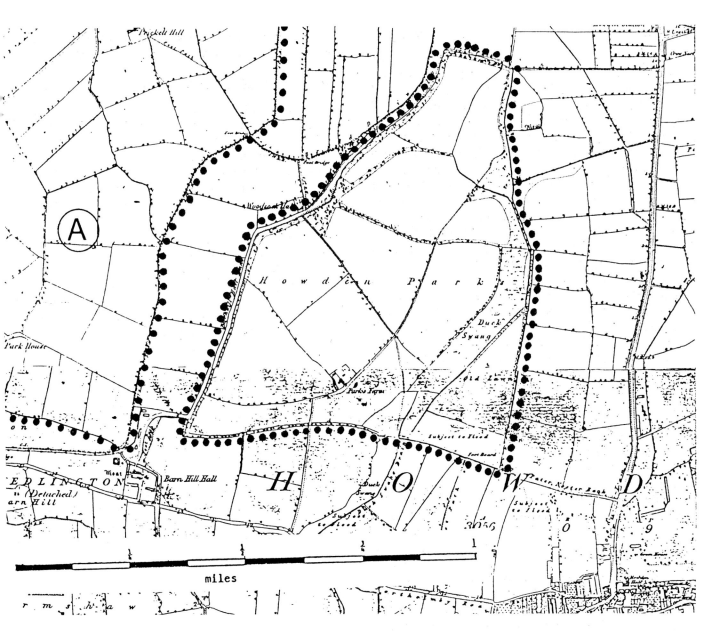

Boundary of medieval park at Howden, superimposed on Ordnance Survey map of 1854.
(A) Newsholme Park.

LECONFIELD
Old Park   TA 025 425
New Park   TA 010 420
Coursing Park   TA 025 432

A park has been established at Leconfield by the Percy family, later Earls of Northumberland, by 1314. An inquisition taken in 1352 refers to a park with deer. The park was enlarged sometime between 1488 and 1517, when 140 acres were enclosed for emparking. The herd of deer was said to number 249 in 1512. The Leconfield estate was forfeited to the Crown in 1537. A survey made the following year described the park as six and a half miles in circumference, and containing 620 fallow deer. The pale was said to be in good repair at this date. Around 1542 Henry VIII took more land into the park and sub-divided it into three separate parks; Old Park, New Park and Coursing Park. A survey of the King's woods taken in 1543 shows that wood from the former monastic parks of Deighton and Escrick was used to repair the pale of the Leconfield Park. By 1554-5 Old Park contained 300 fallow deer and 25 red deer, New Park 400 fallow deer and the Coursing Park 260 fallow deer. The pale of each park was described as good, with plenty of timber available for repairs.

The Leconfield estate was briefly restored to the Percy family, but by 1570 was again in Crown hands when a further survey of the parks was made. The Old Park was still stocked with both fallow and red deer, and the other two parks with fallow deer only. Each park had its own keeper. A fuller survey was made in 1577 when the estate had again been restored to the Percy family. At this date Old Park was said to cover 652 acres, and the pale estimated to be three miles in circumference. The park was stocked with 430 fallow deer and 96 red deer. A timber lodge is mentioned. New Park, also said to be three miles in circumference, covered 362 acres and contained a herd of 180 fallow deer. The pale was described as decayed in several places. A moated brick lodge is mentioned. The Coursing Park was described in the 1577 survey as 'a park of great pleasure for coursing and as it seemeth devised only for that purpose'. This park had a timber lodge and, like that of the New Park, its pale was in a poor state of repair. The acreages of the parks or former parks in the early 17th century were given as 730 acres, 300 acres and 390 acres respectively.

Disparking at Leconfield had taken place by the end of the 16th century. Each park was let to a single tenant by 1603 and by 1616 the parks had been subdivided into numerous closes. Much of the area formerly covered by the parks is now an airfield. The moated site of the manor house known as Leconfield Castle survives, and traces of a bank and ditch along the line of the former park boundary can be seen on the approach to the moated site. Farms mark the sites of two of the park lodges.

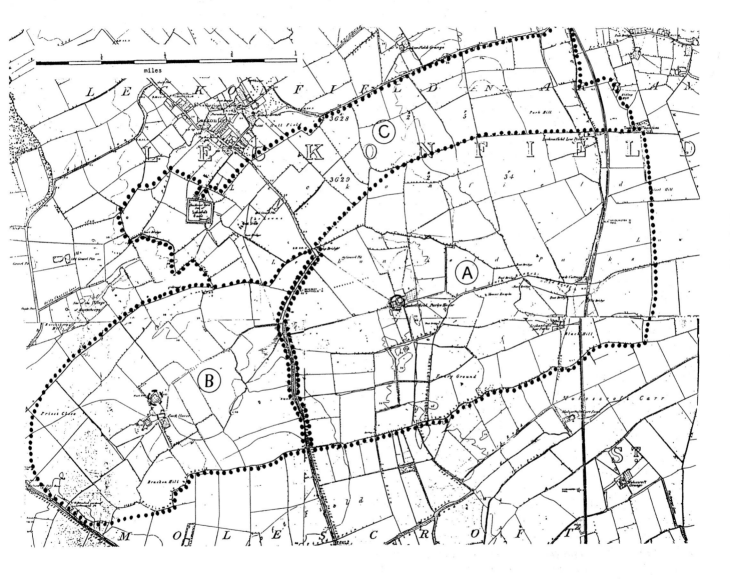

Boundaries of parks at Leconfield, based on a plan of 1616, superimposed on Ordnance Survey map of 1855.
(A) Old Park   (B) New Park   (C) Coursing Park.

LONDESBOROUGH   SE 875 455

There was a park at Londesborough in the medieval period but nothing is known of its history. It had clearly been disparked by the late 16th century; in 1581 reference was made to 'one certain inclosed ground called the park lying between the site [of the manor house] on the west and the highway leading to Beverley on the north and north east ... which said park is now divided into these several closes'. Three of these closes bore the names East Park, West Park and Trusley Park. The Londesborough estate had been in the hands of the Clifford family since 1469, and from 1596 to 1646 there are records of venison being brought into the household from other Clifford estates, as well as in the form of gifts from other local gentry. This suggests that no deer were kept at Londesborough during this period. Payment for the mowing of Park Closes was made in 1646.

In 1643 the Londesborough estate passed by marriage to Richard Boyle, Earl of Cork (who was created Earl of Burlington in 1664) and it would seem that he was responsible for recreating a park at Londesborough. Deer were kept at Londesborough by 1650; amongst the cases brought before the Justices at the East Riding Quarter Sessions in this year was that of a poacher caught stealing a doe from Londesborough Park. References to the paling of the park occur in 1652 and 1656, when hay for the deer is mentioned. There are references to deer in records throughout the 1670s, and in 1679 warrants were issued against 'the people that carried pales out of the park'. By 1698 there were sufficient deer in the park at Londesborough to enable more than 70 of the herd to be transferred to restock Steadhouse Park in the West Riding, which also belonged to the Clifford family. Deer are shown in a Kip and Knyff print of Londesborough of c.1700.

Accounts of 1704 indicate that the park had been extended southwards to take in some land belonging to Easthorpe township by this date. A deer house is mentioned. A small addition was made to the park in 1718,

and from about 1725 a major programme of landscaping was carried out. Further extensions were made to the park in 1729 when £20 was paid for oak pales and rails. Major extensions of c.1738-40 necessitated the depopulation of the small settlement of Easthorpe and the emparking of some 400 acres of agricultural land.

On the death of the 3rd Lord Burlington in 1753, at which date the park covered around 700 acres, the Londesborough estate passed to his son-in-law who succeeded his father as 4th Duke of Devonshire in 1755. The estate at Londesborough was rarely visited during the late 18th and early 19th centuries and the last reference to the keeping of deer is in the game accounts for 1817, shortly before the demolition of Londesborough Hall. The park was divided into farms in 1820. The estate was sold to George Hudson, the 'railway king', in 1845 and he in turn sold it to Lord Albert Denison in 1850. Denison was created Lord Londesborough later that year. A small number of deer were reintroduced at Londesborough early in the present century, possibly as part of the preparations for a royal visit in 1905. The herd was dispersed during the Second World War.

MEAUX (Wawne parish)   TA 093 395

The park which William le Gros had planned to create at Meaux in the 12th century was never completed. In 1151 he granted lands for the founding of an abbey, and the site chosen by the future abbot was at Meaux in Holderness where le Gros had originally planned to establish a park. The park was to have been enclosed by a ditch and bank or wall, and work on digging out the boundary ditch had already commenced. This ditch or dike, which lies on the western side of the abbey site, has retained the name Park Dyke.

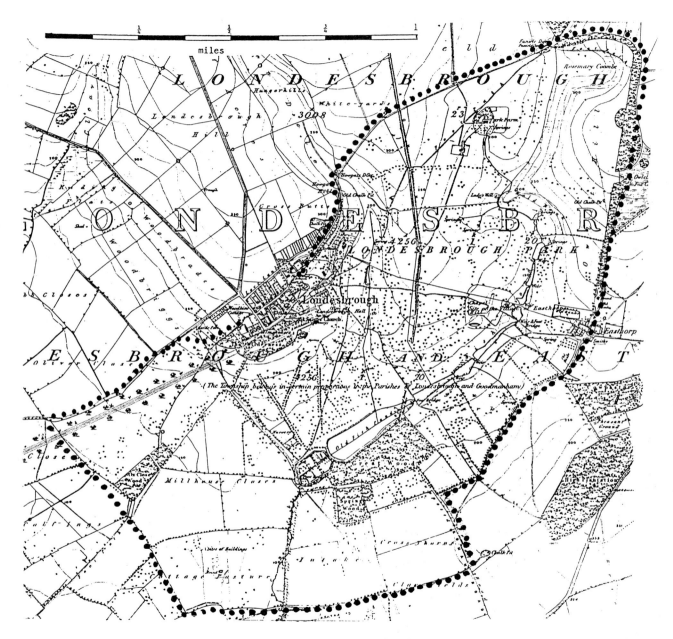

Londesborough Park – boundary based on a plan of 1739, superimposed on Ordnance Survey map of 1855.

METHAM (Howden parish)   SE 807 248

In 1312 it was reported that trespassers had entered the manor of Metham, which had been taken into the hands of the Crown following the death of John de Metham, and that the trespassers had hunted in the park. Nothing further is known of this park.

MOREBY (Stillingfleet parish)   SE 595 430

There appears to have been a small park surrounding Moreby Hall in the Middle Ages, An inquisition taken in 1552 refers to 'the Park' although it is described as a close at this date. An area lying immediately south of Moreby Hall is shown as Old Park on the Ordnance Survey map (six inches to one mile) of 1851.

Deer were kept at Moreby in the mid 18th century. The following advertisement appeared in the York Courant in March 1749:

> To be let. 4 miles south from York, and near the navigable River Ouse Moreby Hall, with the Paddock stock'd with deer (there were about 18 brace) two orchards. Planted with good fruit and bears well, the garden with fish ponds and what ground adjoining to the house there is occasion for — the house may be seen any day, and entered at pleasure and let for any term of years.

It is not known when deer were last kept at Moreby.

NEWSHOLME (Wressle parish)   SE 730 295

A park was created at Newsholme around 1485 when the Earl of Northumberland exchanged certain manors in Surrey and Sussex for the lordship of Newsholme in order to extend his manor at Wressle. Two parks already existed at Wressle, and these have been dealt with separately. The new park at Newsholme was referred to in 1487 when the neighbouring manor of Barnehill was described as lying between the parks of Howden and Newsholme. In 1512

the park contained a stock of 324 deer. By 1538, however, the herd comprised only 91 deer, 17 of which were red deer and the remainder fallow deer. At this date the park was described as three miles in circumference, and the pale was said to be in good repair. The park contained a lodge, which was rebuilt in 1543. The park appears to have suffered neglect at the hands of the Crown, into whose possession it had been taken following the involvement of the Percy family in the Pilgrimage of Grace, and by 1554-5 the stock of deer had dropped to only 23; 18 fallow deer and five red deer. The pale was described as 'clean wasted' and there was no timber available from the park to repair it. The dimensions of the park were given as three-quarters of a mile in length, three-quarters of a mile in breadth across the middle, and half a mile in breadth at the end.

The park was surveyed again in 1570, when it was described as lying a mile and a half from Wressle Castle. It was noted in this survey that the park had once been 'replenished with red deer; but the pale is so decayed of late years, as the deer lie out of the ground and especially in summer, in the corn fields, and are stolen and spoiled, so as at this survey, by the confession of the keeper, there are not above xviii [18] red deer belonging to the ground'. By 1577, when the park was again in the possession of the Percies, the remaining few deer had gone.

The boundaries of the former park, which in 1577 was said to cover 537 acres, are shown on a plan of c.1610. Traces of the line of the park pale have been found in the area, notably near Warp Farm where remnants of a bank cuts across a pasture field.

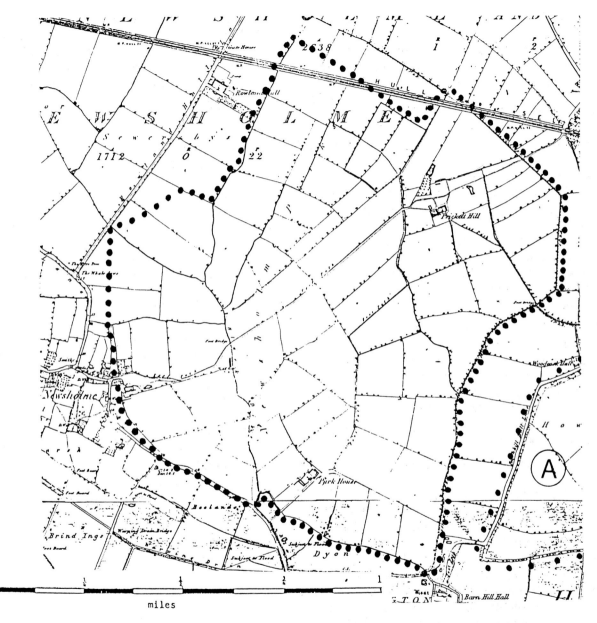

Newsholme Park – boundary based on a plan of c.1610, superimposed on Ordnance Survey map of 1854.
(A) Howden Park.

NORTH DUFFIELD (Skipwith parish)   SE 686 382

A park at North Duffield was mentioned in an assize of 1260 when it was said to have been trespassed in and 'wild beasts' taken. This was said to have occurred shortly after the death of Roger de Thirkelby who had held the manor of North Duffield. Similar cases of trespass in the park are recorded in the 14th century when the manor was held by the Salvain family. In 1474 stints of pasture for swine and horses were let in the park. A close at North Duffield called Old Park was mentioned in 1643 which suggests that disparking may have taken place by this date.

A map of 1760 shows a group of closes lying to the north-west of Duffield Hall called Old Park. Above these lie Park Closes and further north an extensive area of closes is given the name Lawns. The map also shows an enclosed block of land on North Duffield moor called Deer Ruddings.

An area to the south of the village now known as the Parks does not seem to relate to the site of the former deer park.

OSGODBY (Hemingbrough parish)   SE 650 345

A medieval deer park may have surrounded the manor house at Osgodby. In 1591 lands called Long Flatts were described as lying within the park, and deer antlers are reported to have been unearthed in the vicinity of Osgodby Hall.

RICCALL   SE 610 382
(Not to be confused with Riccall Park in Escrick parish)

A park at Riccall belonging to the Bishop of Durham was mentioned in 1311. The episcopal manor house at Riccall was known as Wheel Hall, and accounts relating to the Howdenshire estates of the Bishop of Durham in the late 15th and early 16th centuries include references to both the house and park. A close near Wheel Hall bore the name Park in the 16th century.

RISBY (Rowley parish)   TA 005 355

A park at Risby is shown on Saxton's map of 1577. Evidence presented in connection with a tithe dispute in 1592 suggests that the park had been enclosed forty or fifty years earlier, and it is possible that Sir Ralph Ellerker created the park to coincide with a royal visit in 1540. Extensions to the park were made in the second half of the 16th century, when arable land was destroyed, and the park may have been extended again in the late 17th century when a new house at Risby was built.

Records of the numbers of deer killed at Risby survive for the period 1729-1776. Landscaping took place at Risby in the 1760s and 1770s but soon afterwards Risby Hall was destroyed by fire. It was apparently rebuilt but destroyed after only a short space of time by a second fire. Risby was subsequently abandoned as a place of residence and these events presumably marked the end of the deer park. In 1787 the park was said to cover 106 acres but deer were probably no longer kept in it at this date.

The deer park lay around the site of the original manor house, in the area now known as Cellar Heads.

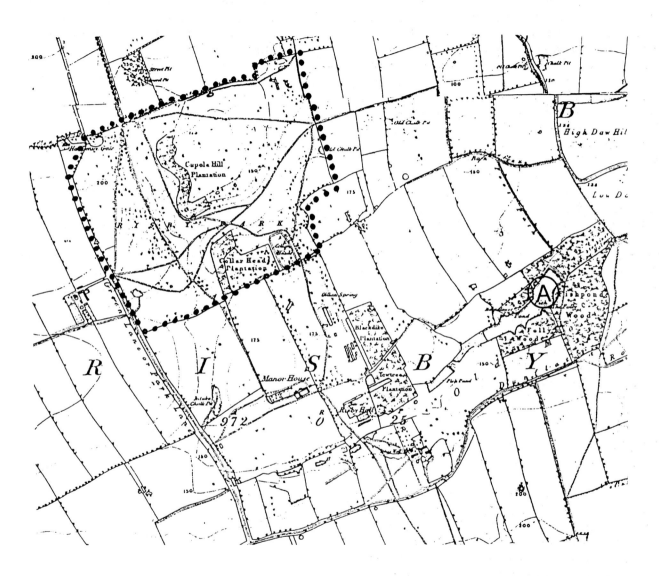

Suggested boundary of medieval park at Risby, superimposed on Ordnance Survey map of 1855.
(A) Location of 18th century landscaped park.

In 1245 a park at Rise belonging to Peter de Fauconberg II was broken into by a group of the count of Aumale's men. They are said to have pursued a stag up to the house, and the daughter of the Fauconberg household was apparently injured as she tried to save the animal. A dispute over rights to hunt in the park had been going on since 1228. The park was mentioned in an inquisition of Walter de Fauconberg's lands taken in 1304, when it was valued at 100 shillings.

The boundaries of Rise Park appear to have been altered on many occasions in its long history. The precise location of the medieval park is unclear, but the incident mentioned above suggests that it lay around the Fauconberg manor house, west of the village. Earthworks in the vicinity of the supposed house site, Black Hall, include a substantial bank which may have formed part of the boundary of the park. It is possible that the park included the areas referred to in the late 16th century as Rise Wood (100 acres) and the Laund (20 acres). A survey of the bounds of the manor of Rise taken in 1624 indicates that the 'Laund' lay on the southern boundary of the parish. By 1716 an area known as Rise Wood was clearly emparked; a plan of that date depicts deer within its boundaries. At this date the park also seems to have included several closes shown to the east of Rise Wood. A tithe document dated 1712 refers to certain grounds lying within the park including Townend Leys which was described as 'in the park and not belonging to Cony Hill'. Cony Hill can be identified from later maps. The area of these closes was known by the name Old Park in 1855.

The principal house at Rise, which had been rebuilt east of the church by 1716, was refronted in 1773 at which date William Bethell, owner of the estate, began his 'alterations'. These seemingly included an alteration to the boundaries of the park, since Jefferys' county survey of 1775 shows the western park boundary dissecting Rise Wood. Capability Brown is said to have drawn up plans for Rise c.1775, but nothing more is known of these, and

there is no evidence to suggest they were ever executed. In 1812 it was said that some 40 acres of Rise Wood had been cleared and taken into the park some years earlier.

Rise Hall was rebuilt in 1815-20, and this may be when a new landscaped park was designed. In 1840 a stock of 300 head were said to occupy about 130 acres of parkland, with 120 acres of adjoining woodland. The number of deer in 1892 was given as 130. The herd was destroyed at the start of the Second World War when the parkland was ploughed up. Some deer appear to have escaped from the park at this time, and wild deer survive in the area.

SCAGGLETHORPE (Settrington parish)   SE 832 728

In 1334 Thomas Ughtred was licensed to empark his woods at Scagglethorpe. No further reference to a park here has been found. The park may have been situated to the west of the manor house site.

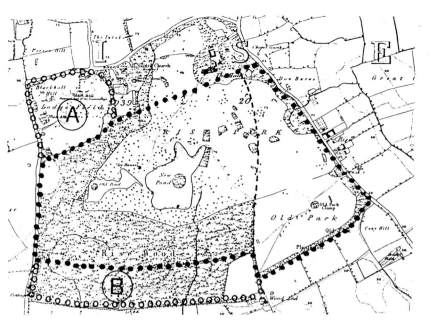

Rise Park in the early 18th century, based on a plan of 1716, superimposed on Ordnance Survey map of 1855.

(A) Blackhall Field, possibly part of medieval park.

(B) Area known as the Laund in 1624.

Late 19th century view of Rise Park, with deer shown close to the house. A deer park at Rise was first recorded in the 13th century.

SCORBOROUGH

TA 018 452

Scorborough was the seat of the Hotham family from the mid 13th century. Eighty acres were reported to have been enclosed for emparking at Scorborough between 1488 and 1517, and this may represent the creation rather than the enlargement of a park, since no earlier reference to a park has been found. The park was extended on the eastern side in the late 16th century. Its boundaries are shown on a plan of Scorborough and Leconfield dated 1616. In 1672 Sir John Hotham presented a brace of fat bucks from the park to the Duke of York (later James II) and in 1683 gifts of venison were offered to the Corporation of Beverley. The Hothams left Scorborough c.1705 following the destruction by fire of their manor house, and it is likely that the deer park was abandoned at this time.

SEATON ROSS

SE 780 400

A survey of the manor of Seaton made in 1343, following the death of William de Roos, mentions 'a little park with deer'. A park keeper was paid the sum of 2d a day to look after the deer. The location of the park is unclear, but it may have been south of the village and north of Seaton Old Hall, in the vicinity of Park Farm.

SETTRINGTON

SE 843 705

The manor of Settrington was held by the Bigod family in the medieval period, but it passed into the hands of the Crown in the early 16th century following the execution of Francis Bigod for his part in the Pilgrimage of Grace. In 1538 the Court of Augmentations leased land at Settrington including a close called the Park. A plan of Settrington dated 1599 shows an area called 'the Parke' lying to the north-east of the manor house, described in the accompanying survey as a close, and comprising part of a tenanted farm. This close of 35 acres may originally have been a small deer park. The distinctive boundaries of the close are still clearly shown on the Ordnance Survey map (six inches to one mile) of 1854, when they contained the parkland surrounding the late 18th century house.

SEWERBY
(Bridlington parish)

Site unknown — possibly in vicinity of TA 203 692

A park at Sewerby was mentioned in 1377 when John de Sewerby leased his manor house and certain lands including a park and a plot of meadow called the Frith. Nothing more is known of the medieval park. A landscaped park was created at Sewerby in the late 18th century.

SPROATLEY   Site unknown - township ref. TA 195 345

In 1301 a reference was made to the King's parks at Burstwick and Sproatley. No further reference to the Sproatley park has been found.

STORWOOD (Thornton parish)

SE 712 439

In 1285 Robert de Roos held from Sir John de Vesci, by knight's service, the manor and park of Storthwaite or Storwood. A park keeper was mentioned in 1343, and there are several accounts of the park being broken into and deer taken in the 13th and 14th centuries. Nothing is known of the later history of the park. An area to the east of the moated site of Storthwaite Hall, described as a close in the 18th century, is still known as the Parks.

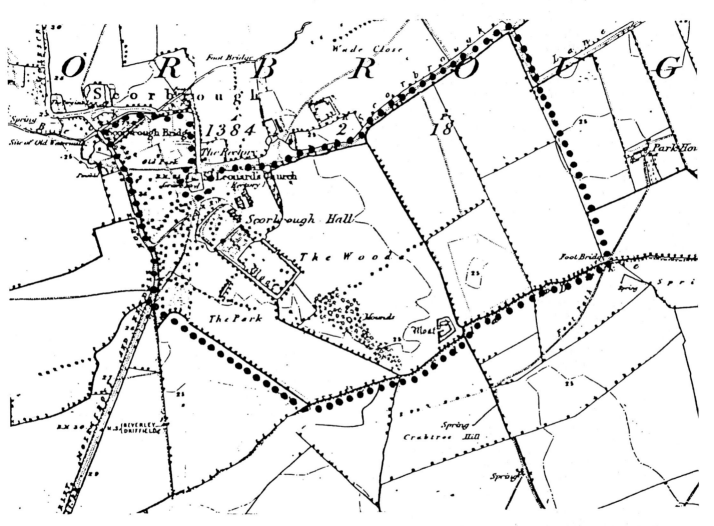

Boundary of Scorborough Park, based on a plan of 1616, superimposed on Ordnance Survey map of 1855.

SUTTON UPON DERWENT

SE 705 470

The manor of Sutton upon Derwent was held by a minor branch of the Percy family and a park is first recorded there in 1280. The park was mentioned again in 1309 when a 'laund' known as Farneforth was also referred to. A survey dated 1367 describes the park as a small wood, and a survey of woods made in 1552 includes a reference to underwood growing in Sutton Park. When the manor of Sutton upon Derwent was surveyed in 1725 it included two areas called Parks, which together totalled over 34 acres, and which were under the same tenancy as the 'Manor Garth'. The medieval park almost certainly lay to the south of the manor house where an area of land still retains the name Park.

SUTTON UPON DERWENT (WOODHOUSE PARK)

SE 732 470

A monastic grange at Woodhouse in Sutton upon Derwent was held by Kirkham Priory in the Middle Ages, and in 1252 an associated park was mentioned. The monastic lands at Woodhouse passed into the hands of the Crown following the dissolution of the priory. A survey of royal woodland made in 1543 includes a reference to timber from Woodhouse Park being used to repair the pale of the deer park at Leconfield.

SWINE

TA 135 357

The park of Robert de Hilton at Swine was mentioned in 1286 when certain people were accused of having trespassed there and taken game. The parson of the church of Sutton was accused of having partaken of venison which had been poached from Swine Park. No further references to the park have been found. A field to the south of Swine village, east of the area known as Hall Crofts, was called Old Park in the mid 19th century.

WHELDRAKE

SE 682 437

No specific documentary evidence to a medieval park at Wheldrake has been found, but in 1625 the manor of Wheldrake included woods called 'Le Parke' and Park Closes are mentioned in the 18th century. Areas to the south of the village are still known as the Parks and Lawn Closes.

WINESTEAD

Old Park   TA 298 237
New Park   TA 300 260

In 1490 Sir Robert Hildyard created or enlarged a park at Winestead. In 1597 the Hildyard manor house was rebuilt on a different site, and a park was apparently created to surround the new house. A map of 1636 describes a 42 acre site in the southern part of the parish and lying to the west of the medieval manor house site as Old Park, and shows an area called New Park surrounding the Tudor house at the northern end of the parish. The parish registers of Winestead record the death in 1629 of Richard Kempe 'keeper many years of Winestead Park'. New Park had apparently been divided into closes by 1669, and part of it ploughed up for arable.

WITHERNWICK (LAMBWATH PARK)

Site unknown — general ref. TA 198 399

In 1275 an order was made concerning all those 'who have chased and taken beasts in the park of Lambwath and fished in the king's fishponds there'. Mention of this park does not occur in any of the records examined which relate to the Crown lands in Holderness around this date, although fishponds at Lambwath are mentioned. The accounts of the Sheriff of Holderness for 1260-1 do, however, include reference to robes for the keeper of Lambwath. Lanes leading south from Withernwick village, known in the mid 19th century as West Lambwath Road and East Lambwath Road, may bear some relationship to the boundaries of the park. The park may have extended

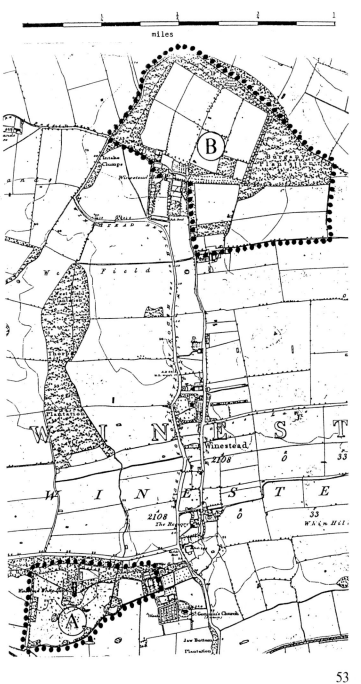

Boundaries of Old and New Parks at Winestead, based on a plan of 1636, superimposed on Ordnance Survey map of 1855.

(A) Old Park.   *(B) New Park.*

53

south-eastward into Aldbrough parish, incorporating the areas known as the Lawns and Lambwath Hill.

WRESSLE
Great Park	SE 710 323
Little Park	SE 707 315

The Percy family, Earls of Northumberland, held two parks at Wressle; a small park adjacent to the castle, and a larger park to the north. A third park, Newsholme Park, was also attached to Wressle manor. This has been dealt with separately.

In 1512 the Little Park at Wressle (said in 1577 to cover just over 11 acres) contained 37 fallow deer, and the larger park, which was known as Great Park, 92 fallow deer and 42 red deer. In the mid 1530s the estate was taken into Crown hands following the Percy family's involvement in the Pilgrimage of Grace, and in 1538 a survey of Wressle manor was made. At this date 50 fallow deer were recorded in the larger park, which was said to measure a mile and a half in circumference. The pale was described as being in good repair. Deer were not mentioned in relation to the smaller park. Between 1542 and 1545 repairs were carried out to the pales of both parks, and also around a 'laund' in Great Park. In a further survey made by the Crown in 1554-5 Wressle Park (the larger park) is described as half a mile in length, a quarter of a mile in breadth, and containing a stock of 66 fallow deer.

The manor of Wressle was briefly restored to the Percies but was forfeited again following the 'Rising of the Northern Earls' in 1569. A further survey was made by the Crown in 1570. The terminology of this survey is confusing since references to the 'Little Park' at Wressle on this occasion refer to the park more usually described as the 'Great Park'. The 'Great Park' mentioned in the survey is Newsholme Park. The park at Wressle is described in the survey as well replenished with fallow deer.

The parks at Wressle were surveyed again in 1577, when the manor had once again been restored to the Percy family. Of the small park around Wressle Castle it was said 'the pale whereof is now in utter decay and no deer within the same'. The larger park, said to cover 184 acres, contained 62 deer of which nine were 'deer of the antler' and ten were white deer. The park pale was said to be in great decay 'and must be repaired of necessity if any deer should be kept therein'. A keeper's lodge, covered with tile and slate, and with stables and outhouses attached, was mentioned. It is not known when deer were last kept in the Great Park, but a map of 1610 shows the park still surrounded by a pale and not yet divided into closes.

Traces of a bank have been found on the north side of Fleet drain, which marks the northern boundary of the larger of the former parks.

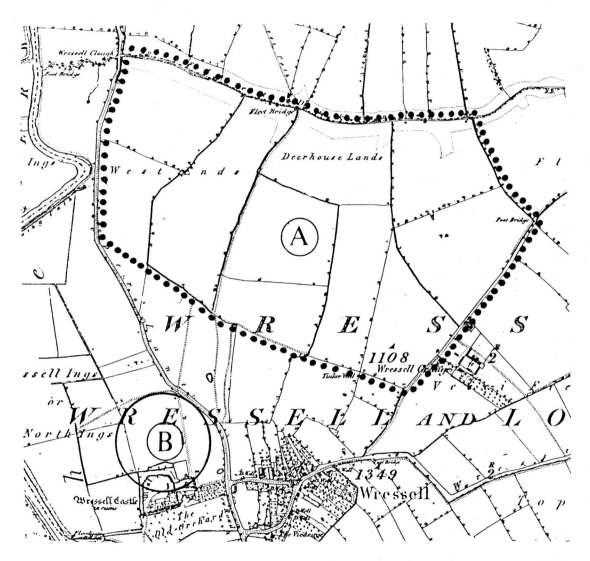

Great Park, Wressle – boundary based on a map of 1610, superimposed on Ordnance Survey map of 1854.
(A) Great Park   (B) Location of Little Park.

Supplementary List

There are many occasions on which field or farm names incorporating the word 'park' or other words sometimes associated with deer parks, such as 'lawn', occur on a map or in a document. Often there is no further documentary evidence available to enable one to decide whether these indicate a former deer park. A comprehensive list of such references has not been attempted, but a selective list of those considered most significant is given below.

BOYNTON

Complaint in 1362 by Peter de Mauley that trespassers 'broke his close, entered his free warren, hunted therein and felled his trees, carried away the trees and other goods as well as hares, conies, pheasants and partridges...'. There is, however, no mention of deer in the enclosure.

CATFOSS (Sigglesthorne parish)

Close called the Parks, 1669; 2 closes called East and West Parks totalling 31 acres, detached from hall site, 1730.

GANTON

Close called 'le Parks' 1587.

GRIMSTON (Garton parish)

Closes called Great Parks adjoining moated site of Grimston Hall, 1928.

HALSHAM

Closes around site of West Halsham manor house known as the Lawns, 1847.

HEDON (vicinity of)

Lands of William de Fortibus at Hedon said to include farm of Pahilsflet (Paulfleet) and herbage of the park of Hawig, 1260.

KILNWICK PERCY

No documentary evidence for a medieval park, but a distinctive boundary bank, typical of those which surrounded many medieval parks, has been traced along the south-east boundary of the later landscaped park.

LAXTON (Howden parish)

Park Close, 1701.

LITTLE HATFIELD (Sigglesthorne parish)

Manor with close called the Park 1694/5; lease of the Park, 1762.

NAFFERTON

Area in vicinity of Nether Hall, which replaced the manor house of the Constable family, known as Park Close 1609 and the Parks, 1642.

NORTH CAVE

In 1628 Sir Thomas Metham was granted a licence to enclose 500 acres for a park at North Cave. There is, however, no evidence to suggest that he made use of this licence; in the mid 18th century the area around Sir George Montgomery Metham's house was described as a bog, devoid of trees. A small landscaped park was laid out c.1769, but there is no evidence that it housed deer.

NORTH FERRIBY

Reference to capital messuage called Ferriby Grange with Park Closes, 1797.

NORTH FRODINGHAM

Manor of North Frodingham with lands including 'le Parke', 1678.

NORTON

Reference in 13th register of Malton Priory; area known as Norton Parks, 1854.

OCTON (Thwing parish)

Reference in Meaux Chronicle to a 'parcum in grangia nostra de Oktona, ad imparcanda averia' — presumably an enclosure for stock rather than for deer.

SCAMPSTON (Rillington parish)

Reference to herbage of park, 1577. A landscaped park was created at Scampston in the 18th century.

SOUTH FRODINGHAM (Owthorne parish)

Meadow and pasture called Red Parrock 1342; closes called Midill Parak, Red Parak and South Parak, 1519; Parrock Meadow, 1723.

SOUTH NEWBALD (North Newbald parish)

Reference to the Parks, 17th century; area in vicinity of site of medieval manor house known as the Park, 1855.

WEST COTTINGWITH (Thorganby parish)

Park Close, 1639.

WHARRAM PERCY

Park referred to in 1324, but probably only a paddock close to the manor house, too small to house deer.

Note on principal primary sources

Much of the original source material for this study was drawn from estate papers. Local collections consulted include those of the families of Maxwell-Constable of Everingham, located at Hull University Library, and of Bethell of Rise and Chichester-Constable of Burton Constable, located at Humberside County Record Office. Material relating to parks held by the Earl of Northumberland (Catton, Leconfield, Newsholme and Wressle) was primarily drawn from the Petworth House Archives, Sussex. Much of the Londesborough material was found in the Bolton Abbey manuscripts at Chatsworth House, and that relating to the parks of the Bishop of Durham at Howden and Riccall in collections located at Durham University. A number of documents held by the Public Record Office, principally royal surveys of the 16th century, were also consulted.

Among the most useful printed primary sources for locating parks were the published calendars of material held by the Public Record Office, in particular those of Fine Rolls, Inquisitions (Miscellaneous and Post-Mortem), Liberate Rolls, Patent Rolls and State Papers Domestic. Relevant volumes from the various record society series, especially those of the Selden Society, Surtees Society and Yorkshire Archaeological Society provided additional material.

Select bibliography

Allison, K. J. (ed) *The Victoria History of the County of York: East Riding* vol 1 (London, 1969); vol 2 (London, 1974); vol 3 (Oxford, 1976); vol 4 (Oxford, 1980); vol 5 (Oxford, 1984)

Allison, K. J. *The East Riding of Yorkshire Landscape* (London, 1976)

Beresford, M. *The Lost Villages of England* (1953, reprinted Gloucester, 1983)

Beresford, M. 'The Lost Villages of Yorkshire: Part II' *Yorkshire Archaeological Journal* vol 38 (1955) pp 44-70

Beresford, M. *History on the Ground* (1957, reprinted Gloucester, 1984)

Cantor, L. (ed) *The English Medieval Landscape* (London, 1982)

Cantor, L. *The Medieval Parks of England: A Gazetteer* (Department of Education, Loughborough University, 1983)
[This useful work contains a list of East Riding parks, to which some amendments are required in the light of the present study. Modifications to the list include the deletion of parks at Burton Agnes, Keyingham, Sherburn and Skipwith, which more detailed research has shown to be based on incorrect source material, or on a misinterpretation of that material. The references cited by Cantor actually relate to parks at Bishop Burton, Burstwick, Sherburn in Elmet (West Riding) and North Duffield respectively.]

Cantor, L. M. & Hatherley, J. 'The Medieval Parks of England' *Geography* vol 64 part 2 (1979) pp 71-85

Cox, J. C. 'The Forest of Ouse and Derwent and other Royal Forests of Yorkshire' *in* T. M. Fallow (ed) *Memorials of Old Yorkshire* (London, 1909) pp 64-76

Crawford, O. G. S. *Archaeology in the Field* (London, 1953)

Fisher, E. J. 'Some Yorkshire Estates of the Percies 1450-1650' (unpublished PhD thesis, Leeds, 1954)

Harris, A. *The Rural Landscape of the East Riding of Yorkshire 1700-1850* (1961, reprinted Wakefield, 1969)

Loughlin, N. & Miller, K. R. *A Survey of Archaeological Sites in Humberside* (Humberside Joint Archaeological Committee, Hull, 1979)

Neave, D. & Waterson, E. *Lost Houses of East Yorkshire* (Georgian Society for East Yorkshire, 1988)

Rackham, O. *Trees and Woodland in the British Landscape* (1976, reprinted London, 1983)

Rackham, O. *The History of the Countryside* (London, 1986)

Roebuck, P. *Constable of Everingham Estate Correspondence 1726-43* Yorkshire Archaeological Society Records Series vol 136 (1976)

Shirley, E. *English Deer Parks* (London, 1867)

Squires, A. E. & Humphrey, W. *The Medieval Parks of Charnwood Forest* (Wymondham, 1986)

Steane, J. M. 'The Medieval Parks of Northamptonshire' *Northamptonshire Past and Present* vol 5, no 7 (1975) pp 211-233

Taylor, C. *Fieldwork in Medieval Archaeology* (London, 1974)

Thirsk, J. (ed) *The Agrarian History of England and Wales* vol 4 (Cambridge, 1967); vol 5, part 2 (Cambridge, 1985)

Whitehead, G. K. *The Deer of Great Britain and Ireland* (London, 1964)